Mini-Cakes

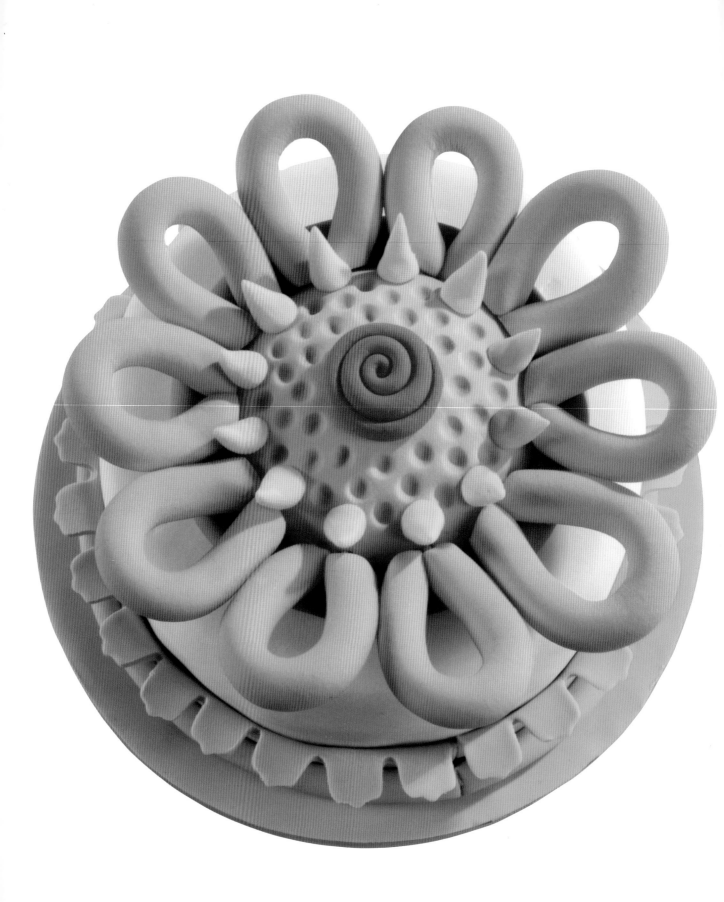

Mini-Cakes

Tiny Treats to Surprise & Delight

Noga Hitron

Photography by Matt Cohen

STERLING

New York / London

www.sterlingpublishing.com

Designed by Eddie Goldfine
Layout by Ariane Rybski
Edited by Sorelle Weinstein
Photography by Matt Cohen

STERLING and the distinctive Sterling logo are registered trademarks of
Sterling Publishing Co., Inc.

Library of Congress Cataloging-in-Publication Data Available

2 4 6 8 10 9 7 5 3 1

Published by Sterling Publishing Co., Inc.
387 Park Avenue South, New York, NY 10016
© 2010 by Penn Publishing Ltd.
Distributed in Canada by Sterling Publishing
^{c}/o Canadian Manda Group, 165 Dufferin Street,
Toronto, Ontario, Canada M6K 3H6
Distributed in the United Kingdom by GMC Distribution Services,
Castle Place, 166 High Street, Lewes, East Sussex, England BN7 1XU
Distributed in Australia by Capricorn Link (Australia) Pty. Ltd.
P.O. Box 704, Windsor, NSW 2756, Australia

Sterling ISBN 978-1-4027-3998-9

For information about custom editions, special sales, premium and
corporate purchases, please contact Sterling Special Sales
Department at 800-805-5489 or specialsales@sterlingpublishing.com.

CONTENTS

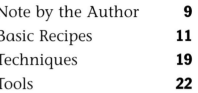

Mini-Cake Designs

Note by the Author

I create cakes that are as appealing to the eye as they are to the tongue. There is nothing I like more than seeing people smile with pleasure and appreciation as they open a box that contains one of my cake designs. Before I began baking professionally, I was a graphic designer. In design, I used contrast, scale, and color to create interesting and appealing works of inspired communication. When I bake, I try to add whimsy, humor, and fun to those elements to concoct cake designs that people enjoy looking at as much as they enjoy eating.

In my previous book, *The Art of Cakes*, I showed my readers how to create cake designs for larger cakes—cakes around 10 inches in diameter. Larger cakes allow you more room to make larger designs with more intricate elements. In my first book, *The Art of Cookies*, I focused on creating cookies that are both beautiful in design and easy to prepare; but because cookies are flat and two-dimensional, you cannot unleash your creativity in the same way that you can with mini-cakes, which are multi-dimensional. In *Mini-Cakes*, I focus on smaller cakes, cakes that measure around 6 inches in diameter. Because mini-cakes are smaller in size, and therefore require smaller amounts, you can spend less time preparing ingredients and materials, and more time thinking of fun and exciting variations of the designs that are presented in this book.

If you want to surprise and delight your loved ones with a personal gift they are unlikely to forget, treat them to a mini-cake. Once you become proficient in the techniques described in this book, you will find that your friends and family will never again be satisfied with a store-bought cake. Instead of running out to the store to buy your father a nondescript chocolate cake for Father's Day, show him how much you treasure him with a "King of All Dads" (page 72). The next time a friend gives birth, don't just settle for a standard card and bunch of flowers—celebrate this joyous occasion by giving the new mom an "It's a Boy!" (page 90) or "It's a Girl!" cake (page 84) and she will be happy that she hasn't started her post-pregnancy diet yet.

I hope that you derive as much pleasure from the designs in this book as I did creating them. Before you prepare a mini-cake, familiarize yourself with the basic recipes, techniques, and tools provided at the beginning of the book and make sure to read the entire recipe from beginning to end. In addition, the high-quality pictures will help simplify the process by providing you with visual aids for each recipe. But above all, remember to have fun and be creative! Enjoy!

Noga Hitron

Basic Recipes
Cakes

The best type of cake for decorating is firm and moist, so that it can be cut and shaped without crumbling. The designs in this book are best suited to cakes that are at least 3 inches high. You can increase the height of a cake pan by lining it with parchment paper, so that the paper extends above the upper rim of the pan. The recipes in this chapter yield enough batter for one 6-inch by 3-inch round cake. You may adjust the quantities according to the size of the cake you want for your designs. When baking these cakes, be sure to adjust the baking time according to your particular oven and to the size of your cake. Higher cakes will require a little more time to bake, while shorter cakes will require a little less time.

Madeira Sponge Cake
* ¾ cup butter or soft margarine, at room temperature
* ¾ cup sugar
* 3 medium eggs
* 2 teaspoons milk or citrus juice
* 2 cups all-purpose flour
* 1 teaspoon baking powder

1. Preheat the oven to 325°F. Grease a 6-inch round cake pan or a 5½-inch square cake pan and line with parchment paper. Make sure the paper extends above the rim of the pan so the cake has room to rise.

2. Cream the butter and sugar until light and fluffy, about 5 minutes if you are using an electric mixer. Add the eggs one at a time, beating well after each addition. Add the milk or juice and mix well until smooth. In a separate bowl, sift the flour and baking powder.

3. Stir the flour mixture into the butter mixture using a wooden spoon, then beat with the mixer until smooth and glossy.

4. Pour the batter into the prepared pan and level the top with a spatula.

5. Place the cake in the center of the oven and bake for 1 hour, or until a toothpick inserted into the center of the cake comes out clean.

6. Remove the cake from the oven and cool for 30 minutes in the pan set on a wire rack. Then turn the cake out onto the wire rack and set aside until completely cooled.

Chocolate Cake

* 5 heaping tablespoons unsweetened cocoa powder
* 1 cup boiling water
* 14 tablespoons butter or margarine, at room temperature
* 1¾ cups sugar
* 2 eggs
* 1 teaspoon rum extract
* 1¾ cups all-purpose flour
* 1 tablespoon baking powder

1. Preheat the oven to 350°F. Grease a 6-inch round cake pan or a 5½-inch square cake pan and line with parchment paper. Make sure the paper extends above the rim of the pan so the cake has room to rise.

2. In a medium bowl, whisk the cocoa into the water until well blended and smooth, then set aside to cool for 5 minutes.

3. Cream the butter and sugar until light and fluffy, about 5 minutes if you are using an electric mixer. Add the eggs and rum extract and beat thoroughly. In a separate bowl, sift the flour and baking powder. Gradually add the flour mixture and the cocoa mixture to the creamed butter and sugar, alternating between flour and cocoa and mixing well after each addition.

4. Pour the batter into the prepared pan and level the top with a spatula.

5. Place the cake in the middle of the oven and bake for 1 hour, or until a toothpick inserted in the center of the cake comes out clean.

6. Remove the cake from the oven and cool for 30 minutes in the pan set on a wire rack. Then turn the cake out onto the wire rack and set aside until completely cooled.

Fruity Cake

* 14 tablespoons butter or margarine, at room temperature
* 2 cups brown sugar
* 3 eggs
* 3 cups all-purpose flour
* 1 teaspoon salt
* 1 teaspoon baking soda
* 1 heaping teaspoon ground cinnamon
* 2 cans peach or pear halves in light syrup, drained and chopped
* $3\frac{1}{2}$ ounces coarsely ground pecans or walnuts

1. Preheat the oven to 350°F. Grease a 6-inch round cake pan or a $5\frac{1}{2}$-inch square cake pan and line with parchment paper. Make sure the paper extends above the rim of the pan so that the cake has room to rise.

2. Cream the butter and brown sugar until light and fluffy, about 5 minutes if you are using an electric mixer. Add the eggs and beat until well blended. In a separate bowl, sift the flour, salt, baking soda, and cinnamon. Drain the peaches, reserving the syrup from one can. Add the flour mixture and the peaches or pears to the creamed butter and sugar, alternating between flour and fruit and mixing well after each addition. Add nuts and mix well.

3. Pour the batter into the prepared pan and level the top with a spatula.

4. Place the cake in the middle of the oven and bake for 1 hour, or until a toothpick inserted in the center of the cake comes out clean.

5. Remove the cake from the oven and pour the reserved syrup over the cake while it is still warm. Let the cake cool on a wire rack for 1 hour, then turn the cake out onto the wire rack and set aside until completely cooled.

Buttercream

Buttercream, jam, chocolate spread, or any other sweet smooth spread provides a delicious surface for applying rolled fondant to your cakes. You can use a variety of ready-made spreads sold at grocery stores and specialty stores, or prepare your own buttercream using the recipe below.

Makes 1½ cups

* ½ cup butter or soft margarine
* ½ teaspoon vanilla extract
* 2 cups confectioners' sugar
* 1 tablespoon milk

1. Cream the butter with an electric mixer. Add the vanilla and mix well. Sift the confectioners' sugar into the bowl, 1 cup at a time, while beating on medium speed. Scrape the sides and bottom of the bowl often with a spatula.

2. When all the sugar has been added, the frosting will appear dry. Add the milk and beat on medium speed until the frosting is light and fluffy.

3. Store the frosting in an airtight container in the refrigerator for up to 2 weeks. You may need to re-whip the frosting before using it after storage.

Rolled Fondant

I recommend using ready-made rolled fondant (sugarpaste), available at many specialty stores and from baking supply catalogs. Rolled fondant usually comes in white or off-white colors, but is also sold pre-colored. To prevent sticking when working with rolled fondant, always work on a dry surface that is lightly covered with cornstarch.

You will find that the quantities of rolled fondant suggested in this book are quite generous. This is because working with small quantities of fondant is difficult, especially when kneading in color. Leftover rolled fondant that is tightly wrapped in plastic wrap and kept in an airtight container can be stored for several months. Keep the rolled fondant in a cool, dry place. Do not refrigerate or freeze.

If the rolled fondant you are working with is particularly hard, try heating it in the microwave for a few seconds (no more than 5 seconds at a time) to soften it.

If you wish to prepare your own rolled fondant, follow the recipe on the opposite page.

Makes 2 pounds

* 1 tablespoon unflavored gelatin
* 3 tablespoons cold water
* $\frac{1}{2}$ cup liquid glucose
* 1 tablespoon glycerin
* 2 tablespoons solid vegetable shortening
* 8 cups sifted confectioners' sugar

1. Put the gelatin in the water and let it stand until it thickens. Place the thickened gelatin into the top of a double boiler or in a bowl set on top of a pan of boiling water and heat well until dissolved. Add the glucose and glycerin to the melted gelatin and mix well. Stir in the shortening and remove from the heat just before it melts completely. Allow the mixture to cool slightly.

2. Place 4 cups of confectioners' sugar in a bowl and make a well in the center. Pour the gelatin mixture into the well and gradually mix in the sugar until the mixture is no longer sticky. Knead in the remaining sugar. The fondant is ready when the sugar is completely incorporated and the mixture does not stick to your hands.

3. Tightly wrap in plastic wrap and store in an airtight container in a cool, dry place. Do not refrigerate or freeze the fondant.

Modeling Paste

Forming many of the shapes and figures in this book requires a modeling paste that is flexible and firm, and that holds its shape both when you are working with it and when it has dried. A suitable modeling paste can be prepared by adding tragacanth gum, a natural thickener, to rolled fondant. Carboxyl Methyl Cellulose (CMC) is a chemical alternative to tragacanth gum, which can be purchased from many specialty stores and in baking supply catalogs. CMC is cheaper and can be stored longer than tragacanth gum.

To prepare 1 pound of modeling paste, lightly dust a dry surface with cornstarch. Sprinkle 2 teaspoons of tragacanth gum or 2 teaspoons of CMC onto 1 pound of rolled fondant. Knead well until smooth. When shaping figures that require a firmer, more stable modeling paste—such as figures that are particularly tall or thin—you may need to add more CMC or tragacanth gum to the fondant you are kneading. Store the modeling paste in an airtight container for at least 1 hour before use.

As with the rolled fondant, the quantities of modeling paste suggested for the designs in this book are quite generous. Leftover modeling paste that is tightly wrapped in plastic wrap and kept in an airtight container can be stored for several months. Store modeling paste in a cool, dry place. Do not refrigerate or freeze modeling paste.

Royal Icing

Royal icing is used for piping letters, dots, and other decorations onto your cake. It can be made with fresh egg whites or meringue powder. Meringue powder can be purchased from many specialty stores and baking supply catalogs.

In general, three consistencies of royal icing are used for decorating:

Thin royal icing resembles thick cream or syrup. To test for thin consistency, draw a knife through the icing and count to ten. If the mark you made disappears, your icing is the proper consistency.

Medium royal icing resembles sour cream. To test for medium consistency, place a spoon on top of the icing and lift up a peak of icing. If the icing forms a soft peak, it is the proper consistency.

Thick royal icing resembles stiffly beaten egg whites. Thick icing should hold a sharp peak.

The recipes in this book require thin consistency icing, unless otherwise stated. If your icing is too thin, add a little confectioners' sugar. If it is too thick, add a little water until the desired consistency is achieved. You may store royal icing made from fresh egg whites for up to 3 days in an airtight container in the refrigerator. Icing made from meringue powder can be stored at room temperature for up to 2 weeks in an airtight container.

Makes 1½ cups

With Fresh Egg
* 1 large egg white
* 1½ cups sifted confectioners' sugar
* 1 tablespoon water

1. Place the egg white and confectioners' sugar in a mixing bowl. Mix on low speed until the mixture has the consistency of thick cream or syrup—about 10 minutes.

2. Test the consistency of the icing as described above. Add water to thin or sugar to thicken, as necessary.

3. Store in an airtight container until ready to use.

With Meringue Powder
* 2 tablespoons water
* 1 tablespoon meringue powder
* 1½ cups sifted confectioners' sugar

1. Place the water in a mixing bowl. Add the meringue powder and stir until the powder is completely blended and free of lumps.

2. Add the confectioners' sugar and mix well on low speed until the mixture has thickened.

3. Test the consistency as described above. Add water to thin or sugar to thicken, as necessary.

4. Store in an airtight container until ready to use.

Techniques

Preparing Your Cake

When preparing the cake designs in this book, you will be more successful if you use a cake that is solid and moist as well as smooth and straight. There are several things that will help you prepare a cake that is suitable for decorating. I recommend that before pouring the batter into your cake pan, you line the pan with parchment paper. This will help the cake come out of the pan smoothly and with a minimal amount of crumbling. It is also important to allow the parchment paper to extend above the rim of the pan to allow the batter sufficient room to rise during the baking process. After your cake has cooled thoroughly on a wire rack, use a sharp serrated knife to level the top of the cake. Before decorating, turn the cake upside down. Your designs will be more successful if you decorate the cake directly on the cake board or on a serving tray, as it is very difficult to move a decorated cake.

Adding Color to Fondant or Modeling Paste

To achieve colors that are both vivid and uniform, I recommend using concentrated gel food coloring. These colors can be purchased from many specialty stores and baking supply catalogs. Gel colors are nontoxic and don't leave a chemical aftertaste. They come in a large variety of colors, which can be mixed to create many more colors. You can design the cakes exactly as they are described and photographed in this book, or personalize them to suit your occasion.

It is possible to buy colored prepared rolled fondant; however, most store-bought fondant is white or off-white in color. If you are preparing your own colored fondant, dip a toothpick into the color gel and add it to the fondant. Knead the fondant well until the color is evenly blended. Add color a little at a time until you have the desired shade. You may want to wear gloves while kneading gel color into fondant, as the colors can stain your hands.

If you need colored modeling paste, I recommend adding color to the rolled fondant prior to preparing the modeling paste by adding CMC or tragacanth gum. Rolled fondant is easier to knead than modeling paste and will result in a more even color. It is important to note, however, that after the addition of CMC or tragacanth gum, colors sometimes may become faded. Therefore, you may need to add extra color to the modeling paste to create strong, vibrant colors.

Gel colors are also used to tint royal icing. Using a toothpick, add the gel color to your icing a little at a time and mix well with a spatula until you achieve the desired shade.

To tint sugar for making sugar molds, mix a little gel color with 2–3 tablespoons of water. Add 1 cup of sugar and mix well until the sugar is evenly colored and has a texture resembling wet sand.

Covering Your Cake

When using rolled fondant to cover cakes, the fondant should be rolled out to $\frac{1}{4}$ inch thick. To determine the area of the rolled-out fondant, you will need to cover your cake, measure the sides and top of the cake across the center, and add 1 inch to each side for trimming. For example, a 10-inch by 3-inch cake will require fondant that is rolled out to a circle 17 inches in diameter $(10 + 3 + 1 + 1 + 1 + 1 = 17)$.

Once the rolled fondant is the correct size and thickness, place the rolling pin in the middle of the rolled fondant. Loosely fold one half of the fondant over the rolling pin and carefully lift the fondant above the center of the cake. Gently lay one half of the fondant onto the cake so that it covers one side of the cake. Lay down the other half to completely cover the cake. Gently smooth the fondant with your hands or with a smoothing tool. Start at the top and work around to the sides, gently expelling all the air pockets. Trim the excess fondant using a pizza cutter or sharp knife.

Choosing a Cake Board

Styrofoam or corrugated cardboard cake boards of various shapes and sizes can be purchased from specialty stores or baking supply catalogs. Some of the designs in this book use cake boards that are covered with paper or foil, while some call for covering the cake board with rolled fondant. When using rolled fondant to cover a cake board, roll the fondant $\frac{1}{8}$ inch thick and cover the board. Be sure to let the covered board dry overnight before positioning the cake.

Working with Rolled Fondant and Modeling Paste

Always work on a clean, dry surface when rolling out or shaping rolled fondant or modeling paste. Use cornstarch to prevent the material from sticking to your hands or the work surface. To stick pieces of rolled fondant or modeling paste together, apply a little water using a small paintbrush. Royal icing can also be used as an adhesive for affixing figures and objects made from modeling paste after they have dried—both to each other and to the cake. Rolled fondant and modeling paste can be stored in a plastic bag in an airtight container according to the manufacturer's instructions.

Supporting Figures

Figures and objects made from modeling paste sometimes require support when using them in cake design. Relatively light figures can usually be supported using pieces of dry spaghetti. If a sturdier support is needed, you may use toothpicks, floral wire, or wooden skewers. Remove all types of non-edible supports immediately before serving the cake.

Storing Your Cakes

Decorated cakes should be stored in a cool, dry place away from direct heat or sunlight. Do not refrigerate or freeze your cake after it has been decorated.

Tools

1. **Bone tool** is used for making indents in rolled fondant and modeling paste (see Figure A). The back of a paintbrush can also be used.

2. **Cutters** are used to cut flowers, circles, stars, and other shapes in rolled fondant or modeling paste. Glass cups, plates, baking pans, or templates can also be used for making shapes (see Figure B).

3. **Decorating bags, couplers, and tips** are used for piping royal icing. You can make your own decorating bags out of rolled parchment paper, or alternatively you can purchase ready-made bags (not shown).

4. **Edible decorating pen** can be used to draw in details on rolled fondant or modeling paste (see Figure H).

5. **Frill cutter** is used to cut frilled edges on rolled fondant or modeling paste (see Figure D).

6. **Frosting knife** is used to spread buttercream frosting on the cake before it is covered with rolled fondant (see Figure F).

7. **Open-curve crimper,** also called a single closed scallop crimper, is used to create textured trims around the edges of cakes. Crimpers come in a variety of shapes and sizes (see Figure C).

8. **Paintbrushes** are used to apply water for affixing rolled fondant and modeling paste, or for painting small details on figures such as eyes, eyebrows, and mouths (see Figure I).

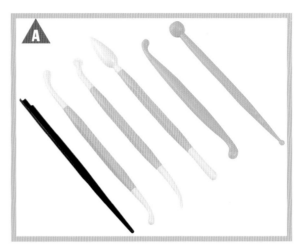

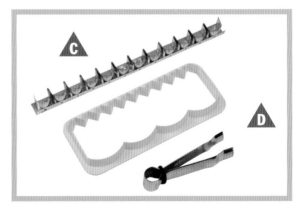

9. **Parchment paper** is used for lining baking pans (not shown).

10. **Pieces of foam** are useful for supporting figures made from modeling paste as they dry (not shown).

11. **Pizza cutter** is used to trim rolled fondant. A sharp knife can also be used, but the rolling edge of the pizza cutter allows for a smoother cut (see Figure G).

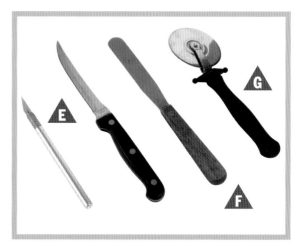

12. **Rolling pins** are used for rolling out rolled fondant or modeling paste. Lined rolling pins are used to create textures surfaces (see Figure J).

13. **Sharp knives** are used to cut various shapes from rolled fondant and modeling paste. Use a serrated knife for trimming cakes before covering (see Figure E).

14. **Spaghetti sticks** are the best type of support for lightweight figures and objects made of modeling paste because they are not too sharp (not shown).

15. **Toothpicks** are perfect for making small marks and for using as stronger supports than spaghetti. Be sure to use high-quality, rounded toothpicks, which don't splinter (not shown).

16. **Wooden skewers** are used for supporting large, heavy figures (not shown).

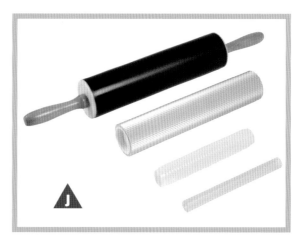

Mini-
Cake
Designs

Spiral Bouquet

Give this fun bouquet to your man and show him that you know how to get funky.

Materials

* 6-inch round cake (pages 11–13)
* 1 batch buttercream (page 14)
* 1 batch royal icing (page 16)

* 12½ ounces green rolled fondant
* 2½ teaspoons CMC
* 5⅓ ounces red modeling paste
* 5⅓ ounces orange modeling paste
* 5⅓ ounces yellow modeling paste
* 5⅓ ounces purple modeling paste
* 5⅓ ounces pink modeling paste
* 9 ounces blue rolled fondant

Tools

* Rolling pin
* 8-inch round cake board
* Pizza cutter or sharp knife
* Decorating bag and coupler
* #3 tip
* 20-inch strip of cloth
* 20-inch by ⅛-inch green satin ribbon

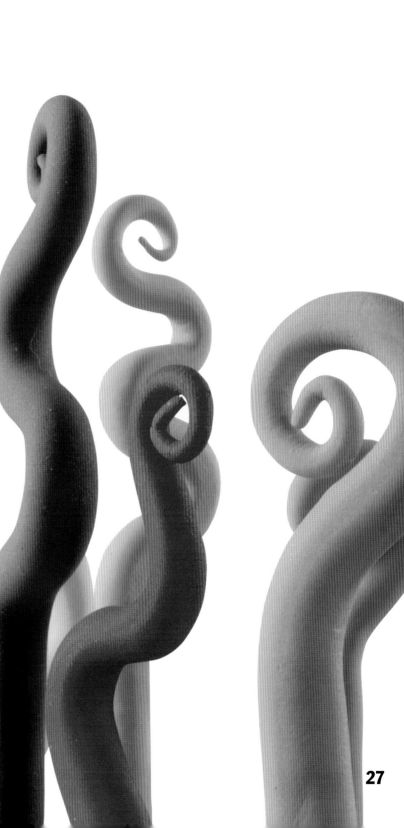

INSTRUCTIONS

Up to one day in advance

1. Roll out 3½ ounces of green fondant. Cover the cake board and trim the excess with a pizza cutter or sharp knife. Set aside to dry.

2. To prepare the spirals, add ½ teaspoon of CMC to each of the colored modeling pastes and knead well. To form the spirals, take a small amount of the colored modeling paste and roll out a long tube, ½ inch wide. Thin out one end of the tube and form different shapes, as shown in the photos. Prepare at least 2 spirals of each color modeling paste. Use a pizza cutter or sharp knife to cut the unbent end of each spiral to make sure that each spiral has a flat surface to stand on. Set aside to dry.

Assemble the cake

3. Carefully set the cake in the center of the cake board. Spread a thick layer of buttercream over the top and sides of the cake. Roll out 9 ounces of green fondant and 9 ounces of blue fondant side by side to form one solid sheet of two-color fondant. Cover the cake so that the seam between the colors is in the center of the cake. Trim the excess using a pizza cutter or sharp knife.

4. Arrange the spirals standing upright around the cake and use a few dots of royal icing to stick them to the sides of the cake. Tie a cloth strip around the base of the spirals and allow them to dry. When dry, remove the cloth strip and tie the green ribbon around the base of the cake to decorate.

29

Mardis Gras Madness

This colorful cake is a Mardi Gras delight. Better than beads, and tastier too.

Materials

* 6-inch round cake (pages 11–13)
* 1 batch buttercream (page 14)

* 5¼ ounces purple modeling paste
* 10½ ounces sky-blue rolled fondant
* 1¾ ounces yellow rolled fondant
* 1¾ ounces lime-green rolled fondant
* 1¾ ounces pink rolled fondant

Tools

* Rolling pin
* 8-inch round cake board
* Pizza cutter or sharp knife
* 3-inch round crinkle cutter

INSTRUCTIONS

Up to one day in advance

1. Thinly roll out the purple modeling paste and cut out 25 $\frac{2}{3}$-inch-wide by 3$\frac{1}{2}$-inch-long strips. Gather up the trimmings and save for later. Roll down one end of each strip as shown in the photo (Figure A). Set aside to dry for at least 3 hours.

Assemble the cake

2. Carefully set the cake in the center of the cake board. Spread a thick layer of buttercream over the top and sides of the cake. Roll out the sky-blue fondant and cover the cake. Trim the excess using a pizza cutter or sharp knife.

3. Roll the yellow fondant into a long tube $\frac{2}{3}$ inch wide. Wrap around the base of the cake and stick using a little water.

4. Roll out the remaining purple modeling paste and use the crinkle cutter to cut out a circle. Center the circle on the top of the cake.

5. Roll the lime-green fondant into 25 balls of different sizes. Form the pink fondant into 10 spirals by rolling a tube and twisting it into a spiral.

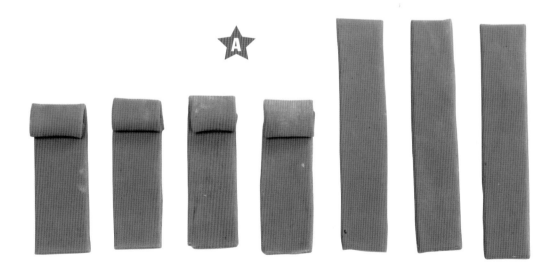

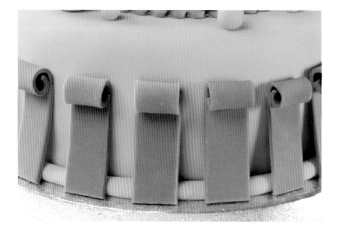

6. Arrange the spirals and balls on top of the cake as shown in the photos and stick in place with a little water (Figure B).

7. Arrange the purple ribbons around the cake standing upright and stick in place using a little water (Figure C).

The Color of Love

A colorful cake to show the one you love your true colors.

Materials

* 6-inch round cake (pages 11–13)
* 1 batch buttercream (page 14)

* 5 ounces turquoise rolled fondant
* 1 batch royal icing tinted green
* 13 ounces orange rolled fondant
* 13 ounces red rolled fondant
* 5½ ounces yellow rolled fondant
* 1 batch royal icing tinted yellow (page 16)

Tools

* Rolling pin
* 8-inch square cake board
* Decorating bag and coupler
* #3 round tip
* Open-curve crimper
* 3 round crinkle cutters—different sizes
* Heart-shaped cutter

INSTRUCTIONS

Up to one day in advance

1. Thinly roll out the turquoise fondant and cover the cake board. Using the #3 piping tip, pipe spirals of green icing around the board. Set aside to dry.

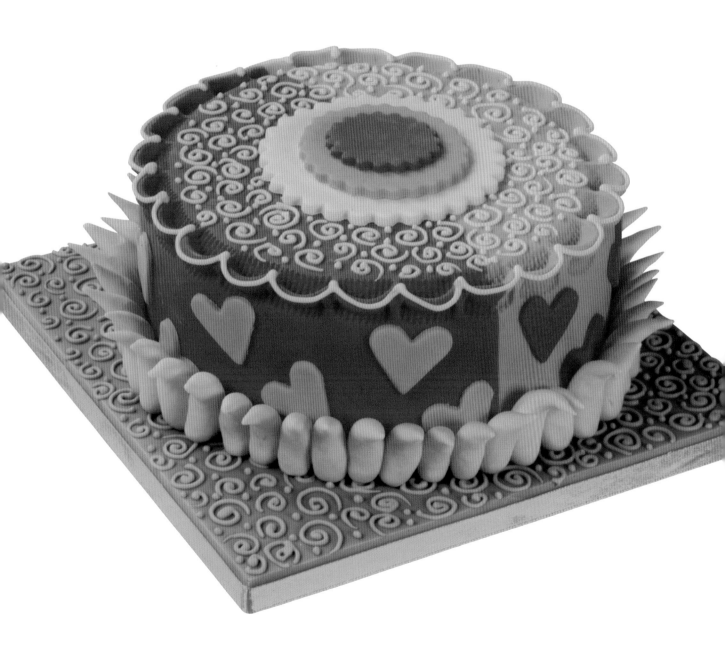

Assemble the cake

2. Carefully set the cake in the center of the cake board. Spread a thick layer of buttercream over the top and sides of the cake. Roll out 9 ounces of orange fondant and 9 ounces of red fondant side by side to form one solid sheet of two-color fondant. Cover the cake so that the seam between the colors is in the center of the cake. Trim the excess using a pizza cutter or sharp knife (Figures A–B).

3. Using the open-curve crimper, crimp along the upper edge of the cake.

4. Roll out 2 ounces of yellow fondant and cut out a 2-inch round with the crinkle cutter. Stick the round to the top of the cake using a little water. Roll out 1¾ ounces of the orange fondant and use a smaller crinkle cutter to cut a circle. Stick it on top of the yellow circle using a little water. Roll out 1½ ounces of the red fondant and use the smallest crinkle cutter to cut a circle. Stick it on top of the orange circle using a little water (Figure C).

5. Roll out the remaining orange and red fondants and use the heart-shaped cutter to cut out small hearts. Use a little water to stick the hearts around the sides of the cake—red hearts on the orange side and orange hearts on the red side (Figure D).

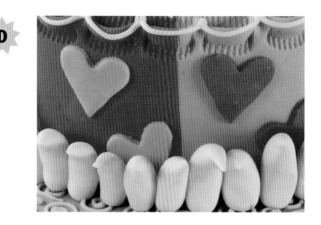

6. Knead the yellow fondant to make it pliable. Form small teardrops and use a little water to stick them side by side around the base of the cake (Figure E).

7. To complete the cake, decorate the crimped edge of the cake with yellow icing and pipe yellow spirals around the top of the cake (Figure F).

Box of Hearts

An abundance of hearts is sweeter than candy on this passionate pastry.

Materials

* 6-inch round cake (pages 11–13)
* 1 batch buttercream (page 14)

* 1 pound white modeling paste
* 9 ounces white rolled fondant
* 2¼ pounds red modeling paste

Tools

* Rolling pin
* 8-inch square cake board
* Pizza cutter or sharp knife
* Lined rolling pin

INSTRUCTIONS

Up to one day in advance

1. Roll out 7 ounces of white modeling paste to a 9½-inch square, about ⅛ inch thick. Cover the cake board. Trim the excess with a pizza cutter or sharp knife. Set aside to dry for 12 hours.

Assemble the cake

2. Roll 3½ ounces of white modeling paste into a thick tube and arrange it around the top edge of the cake (Figure A).

3. Roll out the white fondant and cover the cake. Press the fondant tightly around the center of the cake so that the fondant forms an impression in the center. Trim the excess fondant with a pizza cutter or sharp knife (Figure B).

4. Roll out a 12-inch by 1½-inch strip of white modeling paste. Roll over the fondant with the lined rolling pin. Trim the rectangle so it is exactly 12 inches by 1½ inches. Stick the fondant to the bottom half of the cake using a little water.

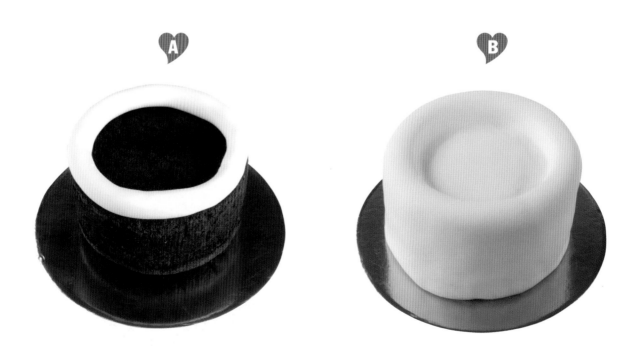

5. Shape ½ ounce of red modeling paste into a teardrop. Use a sharp knife to make a slit at the rounded end of the teardrop, then shape into a heart. Repeat with remaining red modeling paste to make 40 hearts in varying sizes (Figure C).

6. Place the hearts in the center of the cake and arrange them in a pile. Arrange some of the hearts on the cake board around the cake (Figure D).

The Purity of Love

Purity of color and purity of soul go hand in hand in this elegant creation.

Materials
* 6-inch round cake (pages 11–13)
* 1 batch buttercream (page 14)

* 2¼ pounds white modeling paste
* 1 pound white rolled fondant
* 1 batch royal icing (page 16)

Tools
* Rolling pin
* 2 heart-shaped cutters—one large and one small
* 3 tubes in different sizes formed of paper or other stiff material (Figure A)
* Wooden skewer
* 8-inch round cake board

* Pizza cutter or sharp knife
* Decorating bag and coupler
* #2 round tip

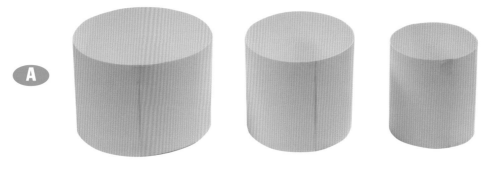

A

INSTRUCTIONS

Up to one day in advance

1. To prepare the hoops, roll out a 12-inch by 1⅛-inch rectangle of white modeling paste. Use the smaller heart-shaped cutter to cut hearts from the modeling paste. Reserve the hearts for later. Space the heart cutouts evenly along the modeling paste. Wrap the modeling paste around a support tube and set aside to dry for 12 hours. Create two more hoops—one 13 inches by 2 inches and one 10 inches by 3 inches (Figures B and C).

2. Form a large heart from ¾ ounce of white modeling paste. Insert a wooden skewer in the center of the heart. Keep upright and set aside to dry.

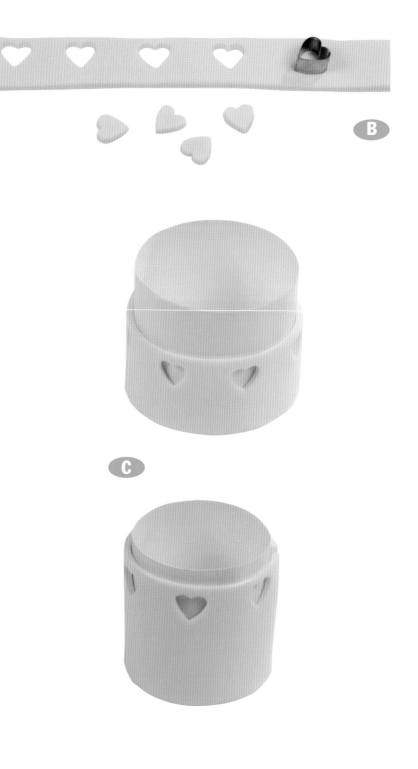

B

C

Assemble the cake

3. Carefully set the cake in the center of the cake board. Spread a thick layer of buttercream over the top and sides of the cake. Roll out 1 pound of white fondant and cover the cake. Use a pizza cutter or sharp knife to trim the excess fondant.

4. Use the #2 tip to pipe royal icing on the bottom of each hoop and stick the hoops to the top of the cake. Place the smallest hoop in the center of the cake first and then place the large ones (Figure D).

D

E

5. Insert the large heart into the center of the small hoop.

6. Use a small amount of white royal icing to stick the 25 hearts side by side around the base of the cake (Figure E).

Heartfelt Hug

If you don't feel like hugging this cute cake, you certainly will enjoy eating it.

Materials

* 5½-inch square cake (pages 11–13)
* 1 batch buttercream (page 14)

* 5⅓ ounces red modeling paste
* 1¾ ounces yellow modeling paste
* 2 ounces pink modeling paste
* 1⅓ ounces flesh-colored modeling paste
* 13 ounces white rolled fondant

Tools

* Rolling pin
* Pieces of sponge or aluminum foil
* Bone tool
* Pieces of dry spaghetti or toothpicks
* 8-inch round cake board
* Pizza cutter or sharp knife
* Frill cutter

INSTRUCTIONS

Up to one day in advance

1. To prepare the red heart, shape the red modeling paste into a teardrop. Make a slit at the rounded end of the teardrop with a sharp knife, then shape the area on either side of the slit to soften the cut. Slightly bend the heart in half as shown and rest it on a sponge or aluminum foil for support. Use the back of a spoon or your fingers to indent a space in the center of the heart for the face. Use the bone tool to indent two spaces for the sleeves on either side of the heart (Figures A and B). Set aside to dry.

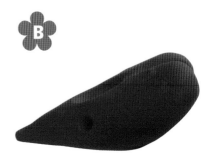

2. To prepare the sleeves, roll a small amount of the yellow modeling paste into a tube. Roll a few small balls of pink modeling paste. Press the pink balls into the sleeve to make polka dots. Gently roll the tube again to inlay the pink modeling paste into the sleeve and make the sleeve smooth. Repeat for the other sleeve. Insert each sleeve into one of the holes on the sides of the heart and insert a small piece of spaghetti through the center of the sleeve and into the heart for support. Form hands from flesh-colored modeling paste and attach them to the sleeves using a small amount of water (Figure C).

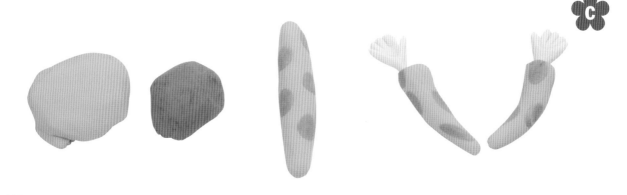

3. Form the face and ears from flesh-colored modeling paste. Attach the ears to the face using a little water. Draw the eyes and the smile using toothpicks or a sharp knife (Figure D). Use a little water to stick the head in the impression in the center of the heart. Form a curl of hair from the yellow modeling paste and attach it to the head using a little water.

Assemble the cake

4. Carefully set the cake in the center of the cake board. Spread a thick layer of buttercream over the top and sides of the cake. Roll out the white fondant and cover the cake. Trim the excess with a pizza cutter or sharp knife.

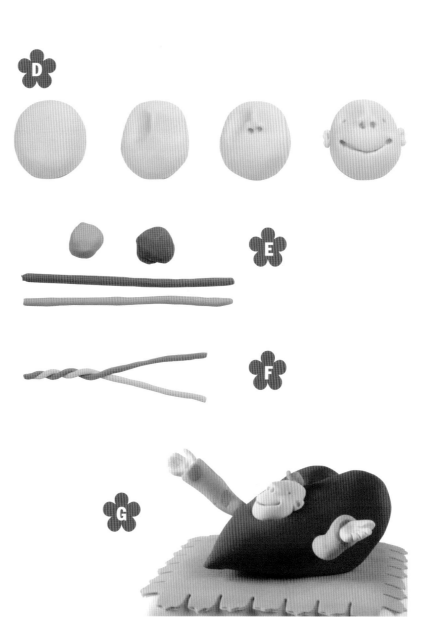

5. Roll out a thin tube of yellow modeling paste and a thin tube of pink modeling paste. Roll the tubes about 24 inches long. Twist them together and stick the braid around the base of the cake using a little water (Figures E and F).

6. Thinly roll out the pink modeling paste. Cut out a 5½-inch square and use the frill cutter to form the frills as shown. Place the pink square on top of the cake and stick with a little water.

7. Place the heart in the center of the pink square on top of the cake (Figure G).

Remove dry spaghetti or toothpicks immediately before slicing cake.

Sweet Summer Splendor

This bold flower is a great gift for a summer garden party.

Materials

* 6-inch round cake (pages 11–13)
* 1 batch buttercream (page 14)

* 18 ounces green modeling paste
* 9 ounces orange modeling paste
* 1 pound white rolled fondant
* 3 ounces light pink modeling paste
* 1¾ ounces purple modeling paste
* 1 ounce dark pink modeling paste
* 1 ounce yellow modeling paste

Tools

* Rolling pin
* 8-inch round cake board
* Toothpicks
* Pizza cutter or sharp knife
* Frill cutter
* Bone tool
* Cut-up sponges or aluminum foil

50

Up to one day in advance

1. *Cake board*—Thinly roll out 7 ounces of the green modeling paste and cover the cake board. Set aside to dry for 12 hours.

2. *Petals*—Form 10 petals using the orange modeling paste by rolling the modeling paste into tubes and folding each tube over to form a petal shape. Insert a toothpick into each petal and set aside to dry (Figure A).

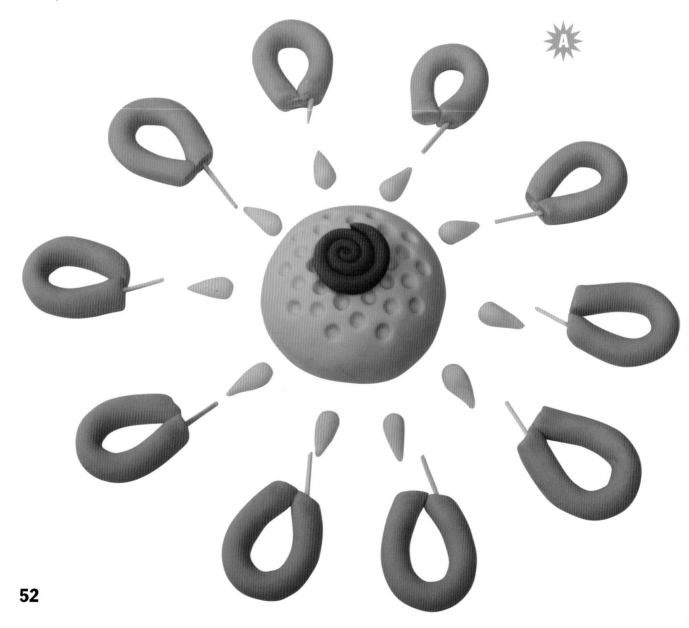

Assemble the cake

3. Carefully set the cake in the center of the cake board. Spread a thick layer of buttercream over the top and sides of the cake. Roll out 1 pound of white rolled fondant onto a flat surface and cover the cake. Use a pizza cutter or sharp knife to trim the excess fondant from the cake.

4. Roll out 7 ounces of the green modeling paste to form a 12-inch by 2½-inch rectangle 1 inch thick. Use the frill cutter to form fringes around the edges of the circle. Using a small amount of water on the bottom edge of the circle, stick the fringed fondant to the base of the cake. Be sure to apply water only to the bottom edge of the circle.

Gently fold down the tops of the fringes evenly around the entire base of the cake (Figure B).

5. Roll out 4 ounces of the green modeling paste into a ½-inch-diameter tube. Using a small amount of water to stick, wrap the tube around the base of the cake (Figure B).

6. Form a dome out of 3 ounces of light pink modeling paste for the center of the cake and use the bone tool to make indentations in the top of the dome. Place the pink dome in the center of the top of the cake and use a small amount of water to hold it in place.

7. Roll out 1³/₄ ounces purple modeling paste into a ¹/₂-inch-diameter tube. Using a small amount of water to stick, wrap the tube around the base of the dome.

8. Roll 1 ounce dark pink modeling paste into a thin tube and coil it into a spiral shape. Using a small amount of water, stick the spiral to the center of the dome (Figure C).

C

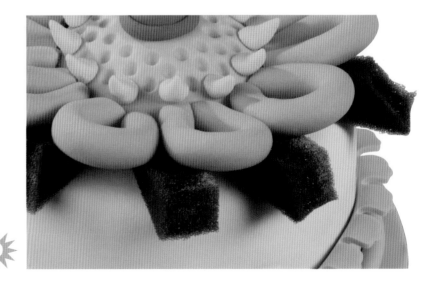

D

9. Insert the orange petals side by side around the dome and use a small amount of water to stick. Support the petals with cut-up sponges or aluminum foil until the modeling paste dries (about 5 hours) (Figure D on page 54).

10. While the petals are drying, finish assembling the flower. Form the yellow modeling paste into small teardrop shapes and attach them to the pink dome using a small amount of water (Figure E).

Excellent Easter Cake

Cheery and colorful, this cake is a delightful Easter gift or springtime treat.

Materials

* 6-inch round cake (pages 11–13)
* 1 batch buttercream (page 14)

* 5¼ ounces white modeling paste
* 7 ounces green modeling paste
* ⅓ ounce pink modeling paste
* ⅓ ounce orange modeling paste
* 10½ ounces white rolled fondant
* 3½ ounces yellow modeling paste
* 1 batch royal icing tinted yellow (page 16)

Tools

* Rolling pin
* 2¾-inch round cutter
* Small leaf-shaped plunger cutter
* Butterfly-shaped cutter
* 18-inch square cake board
* Pizza cutter or sharp knife
* Open-curve crimper
* Lined rolling pin
* Crinkle cutter
* Decorating bag and coupler
* #3 tip
* Toothpicks

INSTRUCTIONS

Up to one day in advance

1. To prepare the petals, roll out the white modeling paste $^3/_4$ inch thick. Use the 2$^3/_4$-inch round cutter to cut out 6 circles. Use the cutter to cut out a crescent from each circle. Set aside to dry for at least 12 hours (Figure A).

2. To prepare the green leaves, thinly roll out the green modeling paste around $^1/_2$ inch thick. Use the plunger cutter to cut out 80 leaves. Gather the excess modeling paste and save for later. Set the leaves aside to dry for several hours (Figure B).

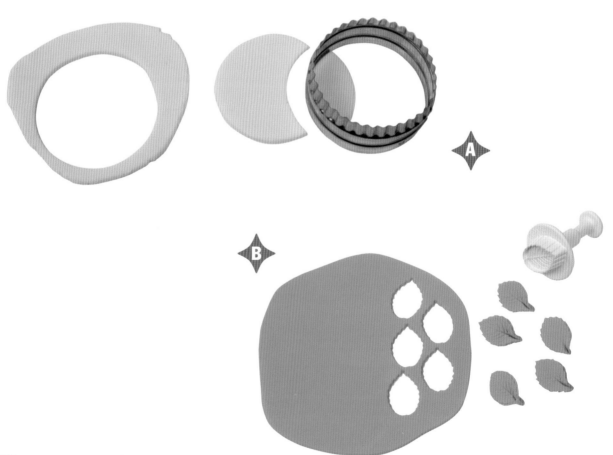

3. Roll out the pink modeling paste. Form small balls of orange modeling paste and distribute them on the pink modeling paste. To inlay the orange circles, gently roll over the modeling paste until the modeling paste is smooth and flat. Use the butterfly-shaped cutter to cut out the butterfly. Gently fold in half and set aside to dry for several hours (Figure C).

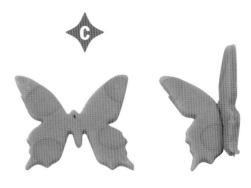

Assemble the cake

4. Carefully set the cake in the center of the cake board. Spread a thick layer of buttercream over the top and sides of the cake. Roll out the white fondant and cover the cake. Trim the excess fondant using a pizza cutter or sharp knife. Use the crimper to crimp around the top edge of the cake.

 D

5. Roll some green modeling paste into a long tube ¾ inch wide, and stick around the base of the cake using a little water.

6. Using a little water, stick the green leaves around the base of the cake side by side in two rows, one row above the other (Figure D).

7. Roll out the yellow modeling paste 1½ inches thick. Roll over the modeling paste with the lined rolling pin, first in one direction and then again at a right angle to the previously created lines. This will form a criss-cross pattern for the center of the daisy. Use the crinkle cutter to cut out a circle from the patterned modeling paste. Carefully center the circle on the top of the cake and stick in place with a little water (Figure E).

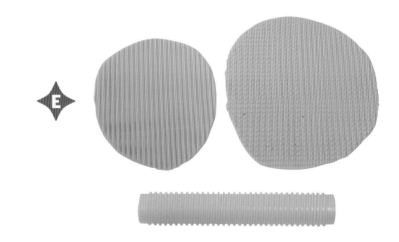

E

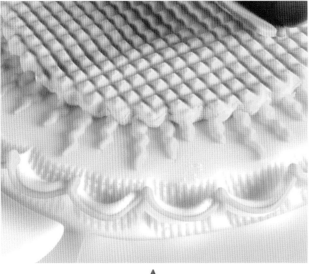

F

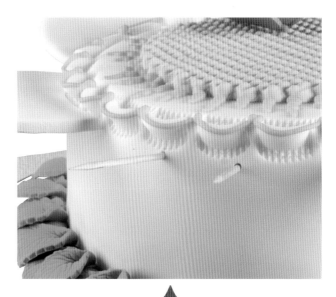

G

8. To complete the cake, decorate the crimped edge of the cake with yellow icing and pipe yellow spirals around the top of the cake (Figure F).

9. Insert toothpicks ⅜ inch from the top of the cake. Pipe a small amount of white icing onto each toothpick and attach the white petals to the toothpicks around the cake (Figure G).

10. Place the butterfly near the center of the cake on the yellow circle (Figure H).

Remove toothpicks immediately before slicing cake.

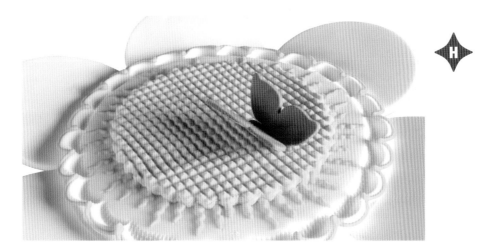

H

61

Fabulous Flowers

A beautiful bounty of bold blossoms adorns this wonderful confection.

Materials

* 6-inch round cake (pages 11–13)
* 1 batch buttercream (page 14)

* 18 ounces green modeling paste
* 3 teaspoons CMC
* 3½ ounces purple modeling paste
* 3½ ounces yellow modeling paste
* 1 batch royal icing (page 16)
* 3½ ounces orange modeling paste
* 3½ ounces red modeling paste
* 3½ ounces pink modeling paste
* 10⅔ ounces white rolled fondant

Tools

* Rolling pin
* 8-inch round cake board
* Pizza cutter or sharp knife
* Floral wire
* Wooden skewers
* Decorating bag and coupler
* #3 round tip

INSTRUCTIONS

Up to one day in advance

1. Roll out 7 ounces of green modeling paste and cover the cake board. Trim the excess with a pizza cutter or sharp knife. Set aside to dry for 12 hours.

2. Prepare 1 large flower and 7 small flowers. To prepare the large flower, roll a long tube from the purple modeling paste, about ⅕ inch thick. Cut it in 5 sections and form teardrop-shaped petals. Form 2 discs, 1 inch round and ⅛ inch thick, from the yellow modeling paste. Roll some red modeling paste into 2 small tubes and form 2 spirals. Stick the spirals to the discs using a little water (Figure A). Cut a wooden skewer 2½ inches long. Wrap it with green modeling paste to form the stem (Figure B). To assemble the flower, place one of the discs on a work surface and carefully arrange the petals (Figure C). Use a little icing to stick the spirals in place. Place the stem under the petals and use a little icing to stick the other disc on top to close the flower. Set aside to dry for 12 hours.

3. Repeat the process using smaller measurements to form 7 smaller flowers using different colors for each flower. For the smaller flowers, you don't need to use a skewer to form the stem—you can use modeling paste alone or insert floral wire if you need more support (Figure D on page 65).

64

Assemble the cake

4. Carefully set the cake in the center of the cake board. Spread a thick layer of buttercream over the top and sides of the cake. Roll out the white fondant and cover the cake. Trim the excess with a pizza cutter or sharp knife.

5. Roll out a long tube of green modeling paste about ³/₄ inch thick. Stick it around the base of the cake using a little water (Figure E).

6. Attach the flowers evenly around the cake on top of the green tube of modeling paste. Use a little water to help them stick to the sides of the cake (Figure E).

7. Roll a small ball of green modeling paste and stick it to the top of the cake in the center using a little water. Insert the large flower into the green ball. Be sure to insert the stem of the large flower at least 1¹/₂ inches into the cake (Figure F).

Remove wooden skewers and floral wire immediately before slicing cake.

65

Queen Mom

Make Mom queen for a day on Mother's Day this year—give her a queenly cake and make her smile.

Materials

* 6-inch round cake (pages 11–13)
* 1 batch buttercream (page 14)

* 7 ounces purple modeling paste
* 5¼ ounces white modeling paste
* Gold food coloring
* 1 pound red rolled fondant
* 3½ ounces flesh-colored modeling paste
* A pinch of blue modeling paste
* 1¾ ounces brown modeling paste
* 1 batch royal icing (page 16)
* Silver-colored candy pearls

Tools

* Rolling pin
* Pieces of sponge or aluminum foil
* Round cutter (for buttons)
* Small paintbrush
* 8-inch square cake board
* Pizza cutter or sharp knife
* Small heart-shaped cutter
* Wooden skewer
* Decorating bag and coupler
* #3 round tip

INSTRUCTIONS

Up to one day in advance

1. To prepare the purple collars, roll out 1¾ ounces purple modeling paste ⅛ inch thick. Cut out the collars using the templates on pages 105 and 106. Form the collars and stand them upright. Support the collars using pieces of sponge or aluminum foil (Figures A and B). Set aside to dry for 2 hours.

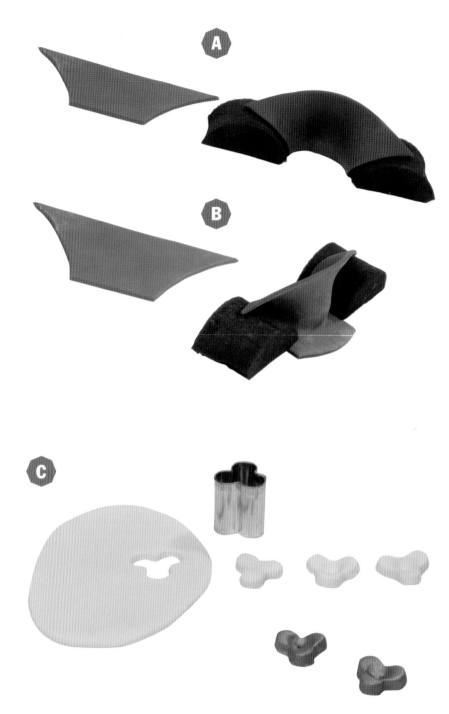

2. Thickly roll out ½ ounce of the white modeling paste. Cut out 4 buttons with the round cutter. Use the template on page 104 to cut out the crown shape from the rolled-out modeling paste. Paint both the crown and the buttons with gold food coloring (Figure C). Set aside to dry for at least 2 hours.

Assemble the cake

3. Carefully set the cake in the center of the cake board. Spread a thick layer of buttercream over the top and sides of the cake. Roll out the red fondant and cover the cake. Trim the excess fondant with a pizza cutter or sharp knife, and keep for later use.

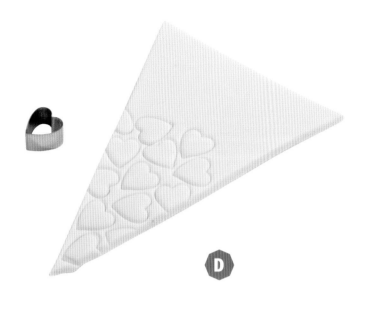

4. Roll out 4 ounces of the white modeling paste and cut out the shirt using the template on page 107. Using the heart-shaped cutter, imprint heart shapes into the shirt. Take care not to press too hard and cut all the way through the fondant (Figure D). Stick the shirt to the front of the cake using a little water.

5. Roll some of the purple modeling paste into a tube and form a 1½-inch ring. Place the ring in the center of the cake and stick using a little water. Stand the collars upright in the center of the cake and use the ring to support them. Use a little water to stick them in place, both to the cake and to the purple ring (Figure E).

F

6. To form the white collar, roll ²/₃ ounce white modeling paste into a cylinder and press one end of the cylinder with your thumbs to indent. Cut out the fringes of the collar and bend them slightly downward as shown in the photo (Figure F). Place the collar next to the purple collars in the center of the cake.

7. Insert a wooden skewer into the center of the white collar so that 2 inches sticks out above the collar.

8. Form the head from flesh-colored modeling paste. Form a nose and ears and attach them to the head using a little water. Form eyes from a pinch of blue modeling paste and form the mouth from red modeling paste as shown in the photos (Figure G). Use the end of a wooden skewer to indent the eyes and stick the blue modeling paste in place with a small amount of water. Attach the mouth to the face using a small amount of water. Stick the head onto the wooden skewer.

H

G

9. Form hair from the brown modeling paste and attach it to the head using a little water. Attach the crown and the buttons using a little water (Figures H, page 70, and I).

10. Decorate the cake using the silver-colored candy pearls. Stick them to the cake using dots of icing.

11. Roll out a 20-inch tube of purple modeling paste and wrap it around the base of the cake and up and around the sides of the shirt (Figure J).

Remove wooden skewer immediately before slicing cake.

71

King of All Dads

Make your dad feel like a king on Father's Day with this royal cake.

Materials

* 6-inch round cake (pages 11–13)
* 1 batch buttercream (page 14)

* 7 ounces red modeling paste
* 5¼ ounces white modeling paste
* Gold food coloring
* 1 pound blue rolled fondant
* 3½ ounces flesh-colored modeling paste

* ⅓ ounce black modeling paste
* Gold-colored candy pearls
* 1 batch royal icing (page 16)

Tools

* Rolling pin
* Pieces of sponge or aluminum foil
* Round cutter (for buttons)
* Small paintbrush
* 8-inch square cake board
* Pizza cutter or sharp knife
* Small star-shaped cutter
* Wooden skewer
* Decorating bag and coupler
* #3 round tip

INSTRUCTIONS

Up to one day in advance

1. To prepare the red collars, roll out 1¾ ounces red modeling paste ⅛ inch thick. Cut out the collars using the template on pages 105 and 106. Form the collars and stand them upright as shown in Figures A and B on page 68. Support the collars using pieces of sponge or aluminum foil. Set aside to dry for 2 hours.

2. Thickly roll out ½ ounce of the white modeling paste. Cut out 4 buttons with the round cutter. Use the template on page 104 to cut out the crown shape from the rolled-out modeling paste. Paint both the crown and the buttons with gold food coloring. Set aside to dry for at least 2 hours.

Assemble the cake

3. Carefully set the cake in the center of the cake board. Spread a thick layer of buttercream over the top and sides of the cake. Roll out the blue fondant and cover the cake. Trim the excess fondant with a pizza cutter or sharp knife.

4. Roll out 4 ounces of the white modeling paste and cut out the shirt using the template on page 107. Using the star-shaped cutter, imprint star shapes into the shirt. Take care not to press too hard and cut all the way through the fondant (Figure A). Stick the shirt to the front of the cake using a little water.

5. Roll some of the red modeling paste into a tube and form a 1½-inch ring. Place the ring in the center of the cake and stick using a little water. Stand the collars upright in the center of the cake and use the ring to support them. Use a little water to stick them in place, both to the cake and to the red ring (Figure B).

A

B

74

6. To form the white collar, roll ²/₃ ounce of white modeling paste into a cylinder and press one end of the cylinder with your thumbs to indent. Cut out the fringes of the collar and bend them slightly downward as shown in Figure F on page 70. Place the collar next to the red collars in the center of the cake.

7. Insert a wooden skewer into the center of the white collar so that 2 inches sticks out above the collar.

8. Form the head from flesh-colored modeling paste. Form a nose and ears and attach them to the head using a little water. Use a sharp knife to cut the mouth and use the end of the wooden skewer to indent the eyes (Figure C). Form two eyeballs from a small amount of black modeling paste and stick them to the face using a small amount of water. Stick the head onto the wooden skewer.

C

D

E

9. Form hair from the black modeling paste and attach it to the head using a little water. Attach the crown and the gold-colored buttons using a little water (Figure D).

10. Decorate the cake using the silver-colored candy pearls. Stick them to the cake using dots of icing (Figure E).

11. Roll out a 20-inch tube of red modeling paste and wrap it around the base of the cake and up and around the sides of the shirt.

Remove wooden skewer immediately before slicing cake.

Birthday Clown

Send in this clown and your child's birthday will be both delightful and delicious.

Materials

* 6-inch round cake (pages 11–13)
* 1 batch buttercream (page 14)

* 7 ounces yellow modeling paste
* 9 ounces orange rolled fondant
* 9 ounces red rolled fondant
* 1¾ ounces white rolled fondant
* 3½ ounces flesh-colored modeling paste
* A pinch of blue modeling paste
* ¼ ounce brown modeling paste
* ½ ounce purple modeling paste

Tools

* Rolling pin
* Sponge pieces or aluminum foil
* 8-inch square cake board
* Pizza cutter or sharp knife
* Pastry brush
* Wooden skewer
* Round cutter (for buttons)

INSTRUCTIONS

One day in advance

1. *Clown collar*—Roll out
   1¾ ounces of yellow
   modeling paste ¾ inch thick.
   Cut out the collar shapes
   using the templates on pages
   108 and 109. Stand the
   collars upright using cut-up
   sponges or aluminum foil for
   support. Set aside to dry for
   2 hours.

Assemble the cake

2. Carefully set the cake in the
   center of the cake board.
   Spread a thick layer of
   buttercream over the top
   and sides of the cake. Roll
   out 9 ounces of orange
   fondant and 9 ounces of red
   fondant side by side to form
   one solid sheet of two-color
   fondant. Cover the cake so
   that the seam between the
   colors is in the center of the
   cake. Cut away the excess
   using a pizza cutter or sharp
   knife and save for later.

3. Roll out the white fondant
   and, using the template on
   page 110, cut out the shirt.

Score lines on the shirt
⅛ inch apart (Figure A).
Use the pastry brush to
brush a small amount of
water to stick the shirt on
the front of the cake in the
center of the fondant.

4. Form a 1½-inch-wide ring
   from some of the yellow
   modeling paste and, using a
   small amount of water, stick
   it on top of the cake in the
   center. Stand the clown
   collars upright in the center
   of the yellow ring so that the

ring supports the collars.
Use a small amount of water
to stick the collars to the
cake (Figure B).

5. To form the white collar, roll
   ⅔ ounce of white modeling
   paste into a cylinder and
   press one end of the cylinder
   with your thumbs to indent.
   Cut out the fringes of the
   collar and bend them slightly
   downward as shown in the
   photo (Figure F on page 70).
   Place the collar next to the
   yellow collars.

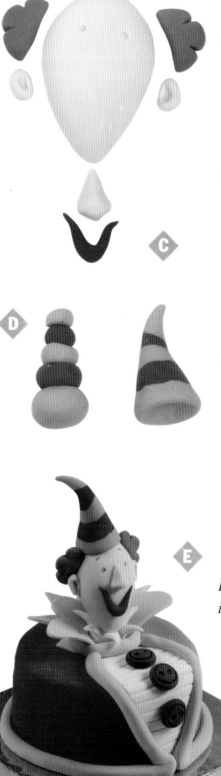

6. Insert a wooden skewer into the cake in the center of the white collar so that the tip protrudes 2 inches above the collar.

7. To make the clown face, use flesh-colored modeling paste to form the shape of the head. Form a mouth from red modeling paste and ears from flesh-colored modeling paste and stick them to the head using a small amount of water (Figure C). Form two eyeballs from blue modeling paste. Use a wooden skewer to indent the eyes and use a small amount of water to stick the eyeballs in place.

8. To make the hat, roll 3 balls of orange modeling paste and 2 balls of red modeling paste. Stack one on top of the other, alternating colors. Gently roll the modeling paste into the shape of the hat (Figure D).

9. Attach the head to the cake by placing it on the wooden skewer. Stick the hat on the clown using a small amount of water.

10. Form brown hair and purple buttons using the brown and purple modeling paste and stick them on head using a small amount of water (Figure E).

11. Roll the rest of the yellow modeling paste into a 20-inch-long tube. Wrap the tube around the base of the cake and up and around the sides of the shirt. Stick using a small amount of water (Figure E).

Remove wooden skewer immediately before slicing cake.

Bon Voyage

This cake is a perfect going-away present for any of your cruising colleagues.

Materials

* 6-inch round cake (pages 11–13)
* 1 batch buttercream (page 14)

* 17½ ounces white sugar
* Orange food coloring
* 1¾ ounces dark blue modeling paste
* 1¾ ounces red modeling paste
* ½ ounce brown modeling paste
* ⅓ ounce flesh-colored modeling paste

* 10½ ounces sky-blue rolled fondant
* 7 ounces lime-green rolled fondant
* 5½ ounces blue rolled fondant

Tools

* 4¾-inch bowl
* Rolling pin
* Toothpick or wooden skewer
* 1 piece dry spaghetti
* 8-inch round cake board
* Pizza cutter or sharp knife

One day in advance

1. Prepare the sugar bowl by mixing the sugar with the food coloring. The sugar should become the consistency of wet sand. Pack the orange sugar into the bowl using a teaspoon. Use the back of the spoon to pack the sugar firmly. Once the sugar has been packed into the bowl, begin to carefully spoon out the center of the bowl. Using a teaspoon, continue to remove sugar until the center of the bowl is hollow and there is about ½ inch of sugar coating the inside of the bowl. Place a flat plate or board on top of the bowl and carefully turn the bowl over onto the plate. Remove the bowl and allow the sugar to dry for 24 hours (Figures A–D).

2. After the sugar is completely dry, prepare the figure of the sitting boy. Roll out a tube of dark blue modeling paste. Fold it over in two to form the legs. Form a cone from the red modeling paste

and attach it to the legs using a little water. At this point, you can sit the figure in the sugar bowl and finish assembling him inside the bowl. Make shoes from the brown modeling paste and sleeves from ½ ounce of the red modeling paste. Attach them to the body using a little water. Form the hands using the flesh-colored modeling paste and use a little water to stick them to the sleeves. Form the head using flesh-colored modeling paste. Form hair from the brown modeling paste and attach to the head using a little water. Draw the face using a toothpick or skewer. Attach the head to the body using a piece of spaghetti and a little water so that it will be securely attached (Figures E and F on page 83).

Assemble the cake

3. Carefully set the cake in the center of the cake board. Spread a thick layer of buttercream over the top and sides of the cake. Roll out the sky-blue fondant and cover the cake. Trim the excess fondant with a pizza cutter or sharp knife.

4. Roll the lime-green fondant into long tubes and form 18 spirals, as in the photo. Stick them side by side to the base of the cake using a little water.

5. Roll a long tube from the blue fondant about ¼ inch thick. Spiral the tube on the top of the cake starting from the center and spiraling outward (Figure G).

6. Use a little water to stick the sugar bowl with the boy inside to the top of the cake in the center of the blue spiral.

Remove dry spaghetti immediately before slicing cake.

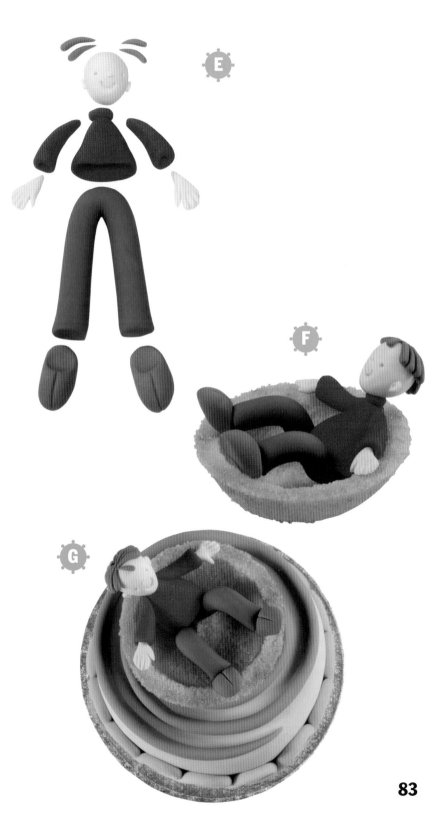

83

It's a Girl!

Sugar and spice and all things nice are definitely what this delicious little girl is made of.

Materials

* 6-inch round cake (pages 11–13)
* 1 batch buttercream (page 14)

* 5⅓ ounces light pink modeling paste
* 1¾ ounces flesh-colored modeling paste
* ¼ ounce dark pink modeling paste
* ¼ ounce orange modeling paste
* 9 ounces dark purple modeling paste
* 1 pound light purple rolled fondant

Tools

* Wooden skewers
* Rolling pin
* Clover cutter
* Toothpicks or pieces of dry spaghetti
* 8-inch round cake board
* Plastic wrap cut into a 6-inch circle
* Pizza cutter or sharp knife
* Pieces of sponge or aluminum foil
* Triangle-shaped cutter

INSTRUCTIONS

Up to one day in advance

1. When making the figure of the baby girl, refer to the photos for help in forming the necessary shapes. Form 1¾ ounces of the light pink modeling paste into an elongated teardrop shape for the body. Cut a line halfway down the body for the legs and form the legs. Fold the legs into a kneeling position (Figure A).

2. Form the two arms with light pink modeling paste and form the two hands with flesh-colored modeling paste. Attach the hands to the arms with a small amount of water (Figures B-C). Attach the arms to the body in a raised position with a small amount of water. Support the arms in position using a toothpick or a piece of dry spaghetti until they dry.

3. Roll out ¼ ounce of dark pink modeling paste and use the clover cutter to cut out the collar (Figure D).

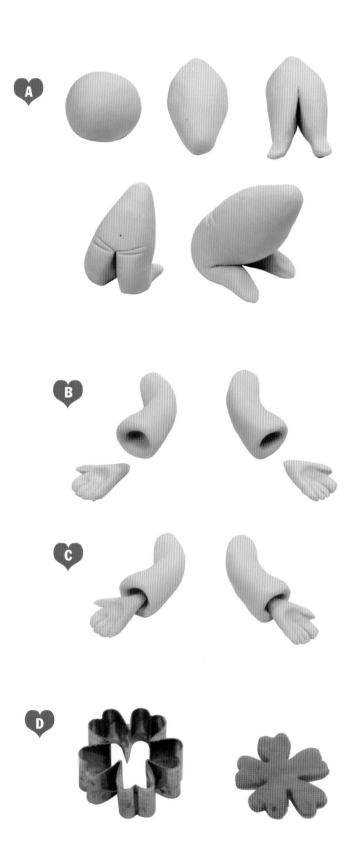

86

4. Form the head, nose, and ears of the baby from the flesh-colored modeling paste. Use the end of a skewer to indent the eyes and mouth. Use the orange modeling paste to form the hair and stick it to the head using a small amount of water (Figure E). Insert a toothpick or piece of spaghetti into the center of the body of the figure and attach the head to the body on top of the toothpick.

5. Prepare the inner layer of the cake at least 2 hours in advance. Carefully set the cake in the center of the cake board. Roll out 1¾ ounces of dark purple modeling paste and cut out a 6-inch circle. Spread a thick layer of buttercream over the top and sides of the cake. Set the purple circle on top of the cake (Figures F and G). Set the cake aside for 2 hours to dry.

6. Place the plastic wrap circle on top of the cake. Roll out the light purple fondant and cover the cake. Trim the excess with a pizza cutter or sharp knife. After smoothing the top and sides of the cake, immediately cut several slices in the top of the fondant from the center outward as shown in the photos. Do not cut all the way to the edge of the cake and be careful not to cut the fondant under the plastic. Carefully lift the edges of the cut triangles and gently form curls by folding them outward as shown in the photos. Support the curls using pieces of sponge or aluminum foil. Use a toothpick or wooden skewer to remove the plastic wrap (Figures H–J). Set aside to dry for about 4 hours.

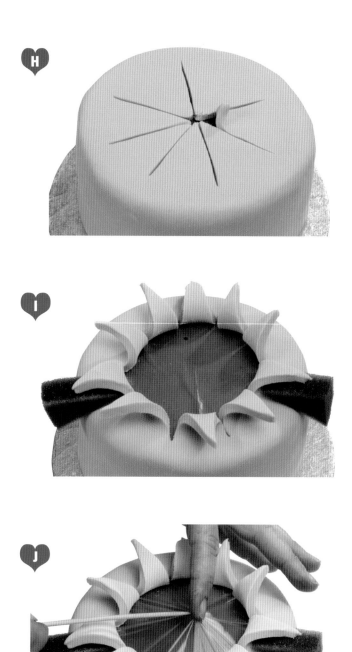

Assemble the cake

7. Roll out the rest of the light pink modeling paste to a 12-inch by 1¼-inch rectangle. Use the triangle-shaped cutter to cut a zigzag pattern along one edge of the rectangle. Use a little water to stick the rectangle around the base of the cake with the zigzag on top.

8. Roll the remaining dark purple modeling paste into a long tube and stick it around the base of the cake.

9. Place the figure in the center of the cake and stick with a little water (Figure K).

Remove the toothpicks or dry spaghetti immediately before slicing cake.

It's a Boy!

Boy oh boy, it's a blessedly delectable, beautifully baked bundle of pure fun.

Materials

* 6-inch round cake (pages 11–13)
* 1 batch buttercream (page 14)

* 5⅓ ounces light green modeling paste
* 1¾ ounces flesh-colored modeling paste
* ¼ ounce dark green modeling paste
* 5⅓ ounces blue modeling paste
* ¼ ounce brown modeling paste
* 1 pound sky-blue rolled fondant

Tools

* Toothpicks or wooden skewers
* 8-inch round cake board
* Clover-shaped cutter
* Rolling pin
* Plastic wrap cut into a 6-inch circle
* Pizza cutter or sharp knife
* Triangle-shaped cutter

INSTRUCTIONS

1. Prepare the baby figure at least 1 hour in advance. Form the light green modeling paste into an extended teardrop shape and insert a toothpick or wooden skewer (Figure A). There is no need to form legs, as the body will be under the "blanket." Form 2 arms from the light green modeling paste and form 2 hands from the flesh-colored modeling paste (Figure B). Attach the hands to the arms and then the arms to the body using a little water so that the arms are supporting the body as if the figure is crawling. Use the clover-shaped cutter to cut the collar from the dark green modeling paste (Figure C). Form the head of the baby from the flesh-colored modeling paste. Use a wooden skewer to indent the eyes. Use a small amount of the blue modeling paste and the dark green modeling paste to form the pacifier. Attach the pacifier with a little water. Form the hair from the brown modeling paste and attach it to the head using a little water (Figure D). Attach the head to the body.

2. Prepare the inner layer of the cake at least 2 hours in advance. Roll out the remaining blue modeling paste and cut out a circle 6 inches in diameter. Spread a thick layer of buttercream over the top and sides of the cake. Set the blue circle on top of cake and let dry for at least 2 hours.

Assemble the cake

3. Place the plastic wrap on top of the blue circle. Roll out the sky-blue rolled fondant and cover the cake. Trim the excess with a pizza cutter or sharp knife. After smoothing the top and sides of the fondant, immediately cut a line in the middle of the fondant on the top of the cake. Be careful to cut gently so that the knife only reaches the plastic wrap and does not cut the fondant underneath. Carefully raise one side of the cut fondant and pull out the plastic wrap with the aid of a toothpick or wooden skewer. Stretch and raise the edges of the cut fondant so that you can insert the baby figure underneath. Carefully insert the figure as if the baby is under a blanket (Figures E and F).

E

F

4. Roll out the remaining light green modeling paste to a 12-inch by 1¼-inch rectangle. Use the triangle-shaped cutter to cut a zigzag pattern along one edge of the rectangle. Use a little water to stick the rectangle around the base of the cake with the zigzag on top.

5. Roll the remaining blue modeling paste into a long tube and stick it around the base of the cake (Figure G).

Remove the toothpicks or wooden skewers immediately before slicing cake.

G

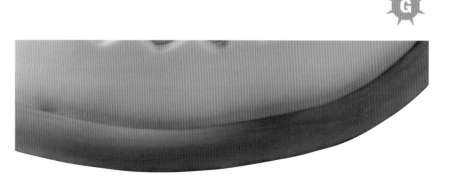

93

Pile of Presents

No need to unwrap these delicious presents. Pop 'em in your mouth and savor the sweetness.

Materials

* 6-inch round cake (pages 11–13)
* 1 batch buttercream (page 14)

* 1¾ ounces pink modeling paste
* 3½ ounces red modeling paste
* 1¾ ounces blue modeling paste
* 1¾ ounces orange modeling paste
* 1¾ ounces yellow modeling paste
* 3½ ounces purple modeling paste
* ⅓ ounce brown modeling paste
* ⅓ ounce flesh-colored modeling paste
* 10⅔ ounces white rolled fondant
* 2¼ ounces pink rolled fondant

Tools

* Rolling pin
* Decorating tool
* Wooden skewer
* 8-inch round cake board
* Pizza cutter or sharp knife

INSTRUCTIONS

Up to one day in advance

1. To prepare the presents, form cubes of modeling paste from each color except flesh-colored. Roll out a small amount of each color of modeling paste. Roll the decorating tool over the modeling paste to create patterns and cut thin strips to use as ribbons for the presents. For each present, wrap a ribbon of a different color around as shown in the photos. Make 15 presents in different sizes and colors (Figures A and B). You may also form colorful balls to add variety to the pile of presents. Set aside to dry for 1 hour.

2. To prepare the figure of the girl, roll a tube of 1⅓ ounces of red modeling paste and fold it over to form the legs. It is a good idea to insert a wooden skewer into one of the legs at this point in order to make it easier to assemble

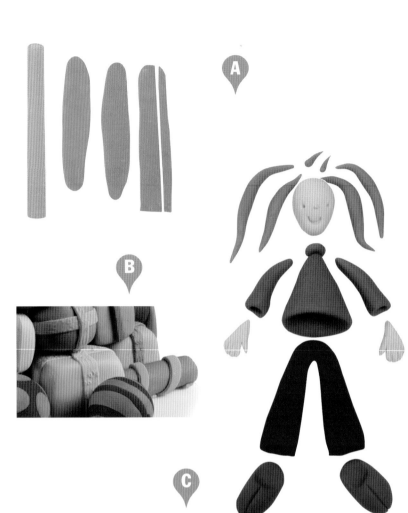

the figure. Divide brown modeling paste in half and shape each half into feet. Form a cone from 1¾ ounces of the purple modeling paste to use for the shirt. Form a small purple coil for the collar. Attach the shirt to the pants. Form the sleeves from ½ ounce purple modeling paste. Form hands from

flesh-colored modeling paste. Attach the hands to the sleeves and the sleeves to the shirt. Form the head from flesh-colored modeling paste and use a skewer to draw the face. Attach the head to the body by placing it on the skewer and sticking it with a little water. Form hair from 1 ounce of orange modeling paste and attach to the head using a little water. Set aside to dry for at least 2 hours (Figure C).

Assemble the cake

3. Carefully set the cake in the center of the cake board. Spread a thick layer of buttercream over the top and sides of the cake. Roll out the white fondant and cover the cake. Trim the excess fondant using a pizza cutter or sharp knife. Roll out a long tube of the pink fondant and stick it around the base of the cake using a little water.

4. Pile the presents on top of the cake and use a little water to stick them together (Figure D).

5. Stand the girl figure next to the pile of presents (Figure D).

Remove wooden skewers immediately before slicing cake.

The Gift of Giving

A beautiful
present with
wrapping "paper"
as sweet as
what's inside.

Materials

* 5½-inch square cake
  (pages 11–13)
* 1 batch buttercream
  (page 14)

* 5 ounces dark pink
  modeling paste
* 13 ounces light pink
  rolled fondant
* 1¾ ounces orange
  modeling paste
* 1¾ ounces yellow
  modeling paste

Tools

* Rolling pin
* Lined rolling pin
* Plastic wrap
* Aluminum foil
  (optional)
* 7-inch square cake
  board
* Medium-sized flower
  cutter
* Pizza cutter or sharp
  knife

INSTRUCTIONS

Two hours in advance

1. Roll out 1¾ ounces of the dark pink modeling paste to a 4-inch by 2-inch rectangle. Using the lined rolling pin, roll over the modeling paste. Cut the modeling paste into ½-inch strips. Fold each strip over a ball of plastic wrap or aluminum foil to form the bows of the ribbon (Figures A and B). Set aside to dry for 2 hours.

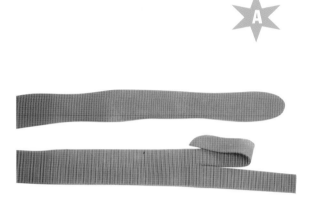

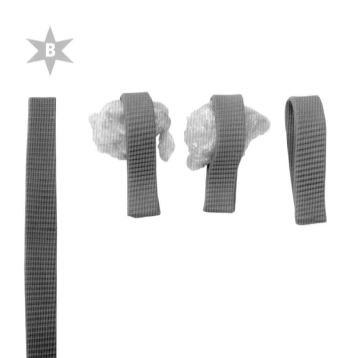

Assemble the cake

2. Carefully set the cake in the center of the cake board. Spread a thick layer of buttercream over the top and sides of the cake.

3. Thinly roll out the light pink fondant to a size that will cover the cake. Cover the fondant with plastic wrap while you are preparing the decorative flowers so that it will not dry out.

4. Thinly roll out 1³/₄ ounces of orange modeling paste. Use the flower cutter to punch out the flowers. Distribute the flowers evenly around the rolled-out light pink fondant. Place a small round dot of yellow modeling paste in the center of each flower (Figure C).

5. To inlay the flowers into the fondant, cover the fondant with a sheet of plastic wrap to prevent drying, and gently roll over the fondant with a rolling pin until the flowers are inlayed (Figure D).

6. Carefully lift the sheet of flowered fondant and cover the cake. Use the pizza cutter or sharp knife to trim the excess.

7. Roll out the remaining dark pink modeling paste to a 10-inch by 2-inch rectangle. Roll over the rectangle with the lined rolling pin. Cut the rectangle into ¹/₂-inch strips and use a little water to stick them around the base of the cake and over the sides like ribbons on a present (Figure E).

8. Use a little water to stick the bows on top of the cake (Figure F).

101

Templates

Queen Mom and
King of All Dads

Crown
Queen Mom

Crown
King of All Dads

Queen Mom and
King of All Dads (continued)

Inner collar
Queen Mom and
King of All Dads

Queen Mom and
King of All Dads (continued)

Outer collar
Queen Mom and
King of All Dads

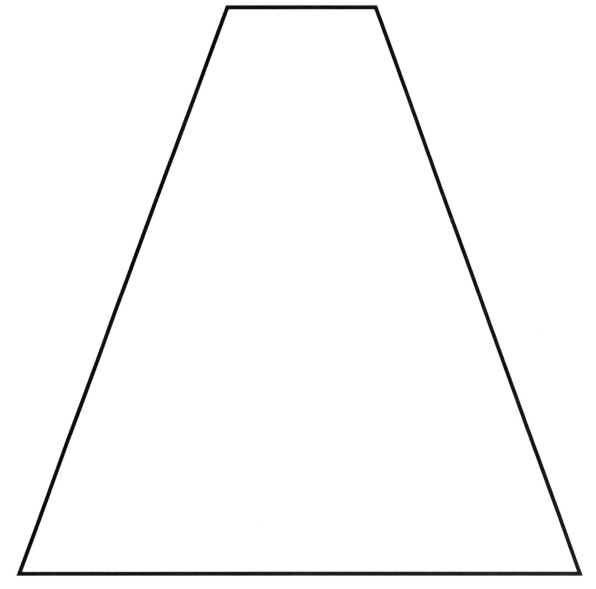

**Shirt
Queen Mom and
King of All Dads**

Birthday Clown

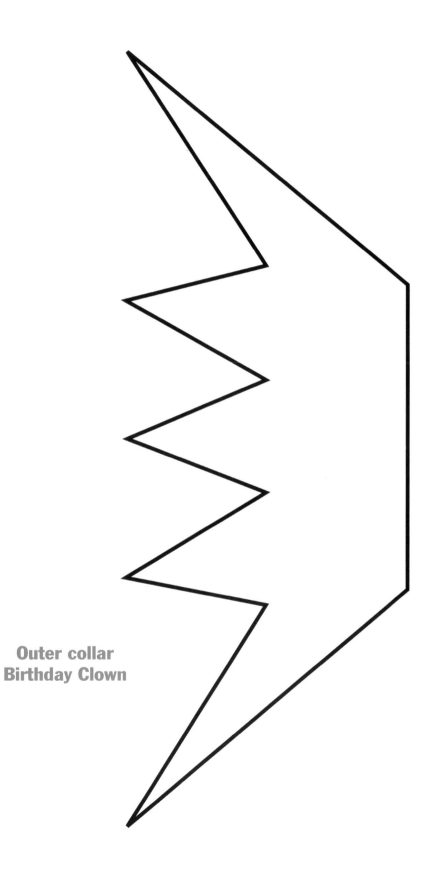

Outer collar
Birthday Clown

Birthday Clown (continued)

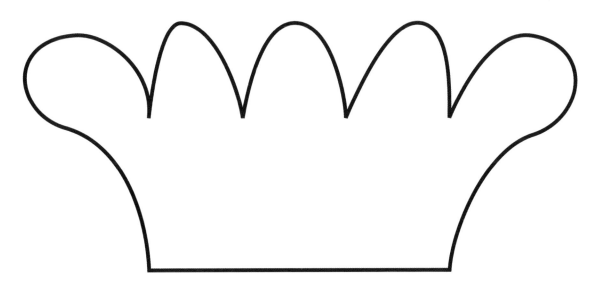

Inner collar
Birthday Clown

Birthday Clown (continued)

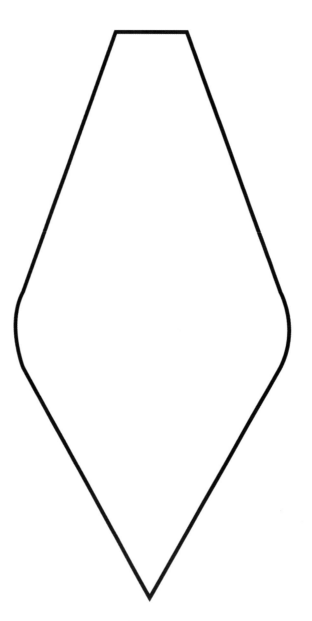

Shirt
Birthday Clown

INDEX